ELK

LIVING WILD

Published by Creative Education and Creative Paperbacks
P.O. Box 227, Mankato, Minnesota 56002
Creative Education and Creative Paperbacks are imprints of The Creative Company
www.thecreativecompany.us

Design and production by Mary Herrmann
Art direction by Rita Marshall
Printed in China

Photographs by Alamy (Premium Stock Photography GmbH, Stephen Saks Photography, Stocktrek Images, Inc., Rosanne Tackaberry), Creative Commons Wikimedia (Austlee, Cherubino, MONGO, NOAA/USGov/Public Domain, Walters Art Museum/Public Domain, Matthew Zalewski), Dreamstime (Chase Dekker, Ingemar Magnusson, Kenny Tong, Twildlife), Flickr (Gerald W. Williams Collection/OSU Special Collections & Archives), iStockphoto (goldistocks, Mickrick, David Parsons, VisualCommunications), Minden Pictures (Donald M. Jones), National Geographic Creative (MICHAEL S. QUINTON), Shutterstock (Nina B, Rod Beverley, BGSmith, Chad Claeyssen, Cindy Creighton, dmvphotos, Dennis W. Donohue, Bob Hosea, Ronnie Howard, Lorraine Logan, Martin Mecnarowski, Holly Michele, Chris Moody, David Osborn, Pritha Photography, Brian Sallee, Zina Seletskaya, Paul Staniszewski, TheGreenMan, Tom Tietz, Wollertz, zschnepf)

Library of Congress Cataloging-in-Publication Data
Names: Gish, Melissa, author.
Title: Elk / Melissa Gish.
Series: Living wild.
Includes bibliographical references and index.
Summary: A look at elk, including their habitats, physical characteristics such as their camouflaging pelage, behaviors, relationships with humans, and the negative effects of climate change on these magnificent deer today.
Identifiers: LCCN 2016036680 / ISBN 978-1-60818-829-1 (hardcover) / ISBN 978-1-62832-432-7 (pbk) / ISBN 978-1-56660-877-0 (eBook)
Subjects: LCSH: Elk—Juvenile literature.
Classification: LCC QL737.U55 G568 2017 / DDC 599.65/7—dc23

CCSS: RI.5.1, 2, 3, 8; RST.6-8.1, 2, 5, 6, 8; RH.6-8.3, 4, 5, 6, 7, 8

First Edition HC 9 8 7 6 5 4 3 2 1
First Edition PBK 9 8 7 6 5 4 3 2 1

CREATIVE EDUCATION • CREATIVE PAPERBACKS

ELK

Melissa Gish

In Washington's Okanogan-Wenatchee National

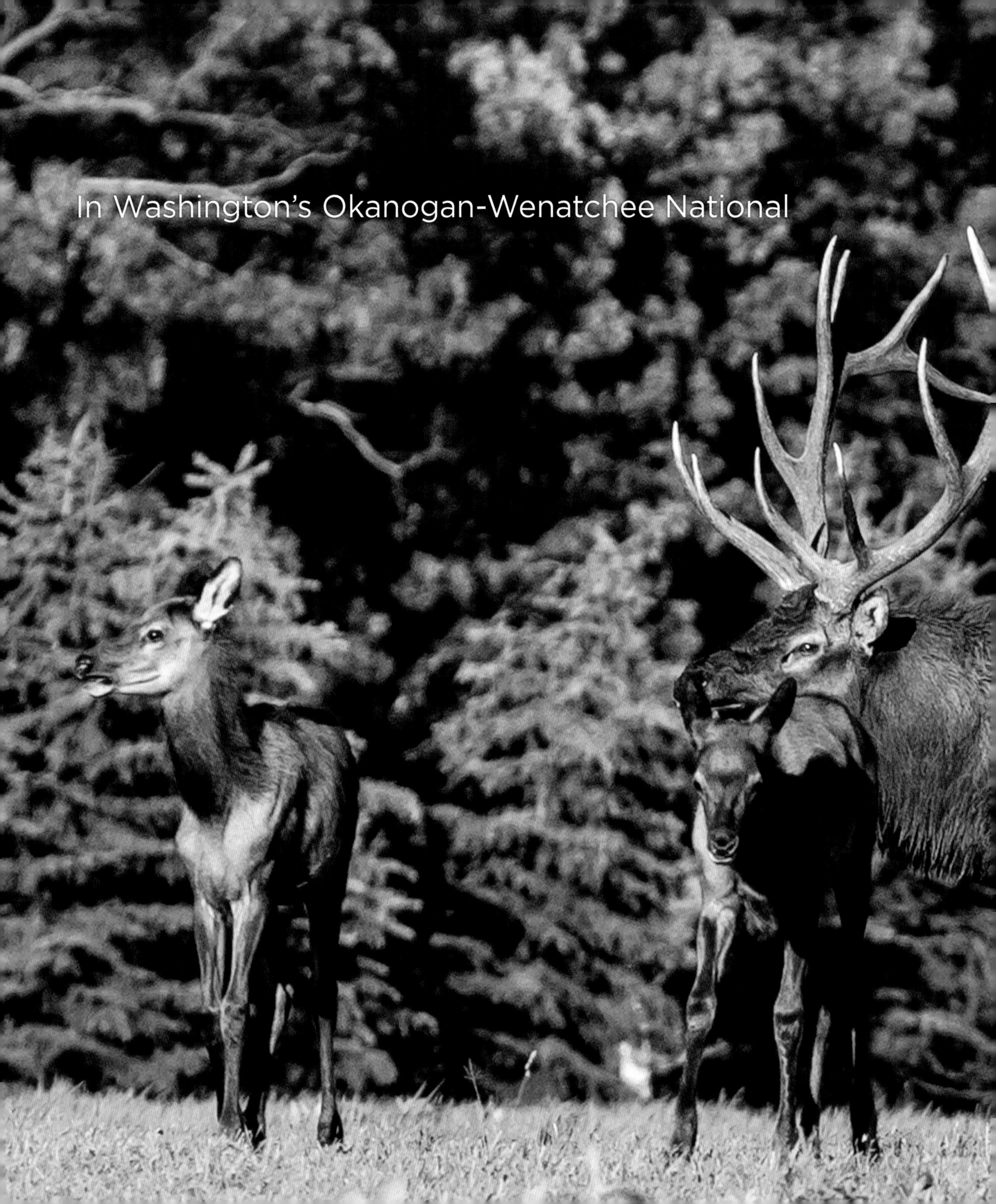

Forest, a herd of elk grazes in a meadow.

In Washington's Okanogan-Wenatchee National Forest, a herd of elk grazes in a meadow. The spring rains have fed the grasses and shrubs in the eastern foothills of the Cascade Mountains. The elk stand knee-deep in bluebunch wheatgrass. They scan the nearby tree line, watching for predators. Every so often, the elk lower their heads and shear off the tender tops of the grass. Young elk stand close to their mothers.

One youngster dozes at its mother's feet. Suddenly, a shape emerges from the forest: a coyote. The elk freeze, waiting for a signal. The herd's leader, a big male, turns toward the tree line, his eyes fixed on the intruder. The coyote's eyes dart to the young elk and then back to the big male. Even the hungriest coyote is no match for an adult elk. The coyote turns away, and the herd resumes grazing.

WHERE IN THE WORLD THEY LIVE

■ **Roosevelt Elk**
Alaska to Oregon

□ **Rocky Mountain Elk**
western United States
and Canada

■ **Manitoban Elk**
midwestern United
States and western
Canada

■ **Tule Elk**
California

Naturally found only in North America, thriving populations of four elk
subspecies reside in forests, mountains, grasslands, and marshes alike.
Roosevelt, or Olympic, elk are named after president Theodore Roosevelt,
who established Olympic National Park in Washington. Rocky Mountain
elk are named for their mountainous habitat and Manitoban elk for their
grassland territory, while tule elk are named for a plant common to the
California marshes they inhabit. The colored squares represent areas
where the elk subspecies are found in the wild today.

OH, DEER!

European moose, once known as elch, *are found in northern woodlands from Norway to Siberia.*

T he elk is the second-largest member of the Cervidae, or deer, family. There are four living subspecies of elk. The Roosevelt elk—also known as the Olympic elk—is found from the rainforests of Oregon to Alaska. The Rocky Mountain elk lives in the Rockies and adjacent mountain ranges of the western United States and Canada. The Manitoban elk roams the prairies of the Midwestern states and Canada's prairie provinces of Alberta, Saskatchewan, and Manitoba. The tule elk inhabits grasslands and marshes from California's Central Valley to its coast.

In the central U.S., Shawnee Indians called elk *wapiti*, which means "white rump" and refers to the elk's coloration. In 1806, American naturalist and physician Benjamin Smith Barton, hearing the Shawnee name, gave the elk the scientific name *Cervus wapiti*. However, this name conflicted with *Cervus canadensis*, the scientific name assigned to elk by German naturalist Johann Erxleben in 1777. Erxleben's name is still in use today. The common name elk comes from the German *elch*, a name originally given to moose in Europe. When settlers first saw elk in

Weighing more than 700 pounds (318 kg), sambar deer are the third-largest members of the deer family, after moose and elk.

Cowbirds have a symbiotic relationship with elk, picking off insects and **parasites** and getting a meal in the process.

the New World, they equated the tall beasts with European moose and called them by the same name. Today, elk and moose are still known by the same name in Europe.

Despite being related, deer, moose, and elk all vary in appearance. There are dozens of Cervidae species, from South America's 22-pound (10 kg) southern pudú—the smallest deer in the world—to the common white-tailed deer of North America to the moose of the Northern Hemisphere. Elk were once believed to be a subspecies of red deer, which are native to Europe, but **genetic** studies in 2004 set elk apart from red deer. Elk also resemble sambar deer, which are found in Southeast Asia, southern India, and southern China.

Elk are mammals. All mammals produce milk to feed their young and, with the exceptions of the egg-laying platypuses and echidnas of Australia, give birth to live offspring. Mammals are also warm-blooded. This means that their bodies try to maintain a healthy, constant temperature that is usually warmer than their surroundings.

An elk has two coats of fur, or pelage, each year. During the cold winter months, the elk's pelage has two layers. Close to the body is a coat of thick, curly underfur. On top

Small flocks of cowbirds may follow elk, occasionally landing on the elk to pick insects from their coats.

Covered in soft velvet, growing antlers are rich with blood, slightly bendable like human noses, and rounded at the tips.

of the underfur are long, coarse guard hairs. These hollow hairs trap warm air, **insulating** the elk from the cold. Both male and female elk have thick, dark manes covering their necks. The light tan winter coat over the rest of the body provides camouflage, helping elk blend in with dried grasses.

Beginning in March, when the days get longer, the winter coat starts falling off and is replaced by a new coat. To loosen their winter pelage, elk lick themselves and rub against trees and rocks. The mane also falls off, leaving the elk's summer coat short, glossy, and darkly copper-colored. This coat provides camouflage in tall grasses and wooded areas. As the days get shorter in September, the winter coat returns. A whitish patch of fur covers the elk's rump year round.

The Roosevelt elk is the largest subspecies. Male elk, called bulls, may weigh 1,000 pounds (454 kg) and stand 5 feet (1.5 m) tall at the shoulder. They may grow to eight feet (2.4 m) long from nose to tail. Bull Manitoban elk are just as big but rarely weigh more than 770 pounds (349 kg). Rocky Mountain bulls may weigh up to 700 pounds (318 kg), while bull tule elk typically top out at 400 pounds (181 kg). Female elk, called cows, are about

An elk's light-colored rump breaks up the outline of its dark body, making it more difficult for predators to see.

Because bulls retain their antlers until spring, they are able to practice playful, nonaggressive sparring all winter.

Antlers are some of the fastest-growing tissues in the animal kingdom, growing several inches per week.

the same height as bulls, but they are not as bulky and therefore weigh 25 to 30 percent less than bulls.

Bull elk have antlers, which are sometimes confused with horns. Horns are made of bone and covered with a hard tissue called keratin. Goats, sheep, and many other hoofed animals have horns, which, unless broken, do not fall off. Antlers are **appendages** that grow from two points on the top of the skull called pedicles. A pair of antlers is known as a rack.

Antlers begin as little knobs in the spring of each year. As they grow, their shape becomes more complex, and a number of prongs develop. A layer of soft tissue called velvet covers the antlers. The velvet is filled with blood vessels that deliver **nutrients** to the developing rack. After about four months, when the antlers have reached their full size, the velvet begins to dry up and loosen from the bone beneath it. Bulls rub their antlers against trees to shed the velvet.

The antlers fall off at the end of winter. The pedicles scab over and heal quickly. Within a couple of months, the process begins again, with the antlers growing faster and larger each year. By the time he is eight years old, a bull may have his most impressive rack. The Rocky

White hairs that spring up on an elk's pelage typically do not appear in the same place every year.

After losing their first set of teeth, elk grow all their permanent teeth by the time they are three years old.

Ivories are useful in telling an elk's age; since elk wear down their ivories as they eat, older elk have shorter ivories.

Mountain elk has the largest antlers of all the subspecies. Its rack can weigh up to 40 pounds (18.1 kg), and the central beams can reach 5 feet (1.5 m) in length with up to 6 sharp prongs branching from each beam.

Elk eat grass, shrubs, twigs, and even small trees. Digesting such woody food requires a special stomach with four chambers. Food enters the first chamber, called the rumen, where bacteria and acids soften it. Then the food is regurgitated, or brought back up to the mouth. This food mass, called cud, is chewed again. When it is swallowed, the cud passes through all four stomach chambers to be fully digested. Elk share this cud-chewing trait with cows, sheep, giraffes, llamas, bison, and many other hoofed mammals.

Elk have 34 teeth, but no front teeth in the upper jaw. They rip plants using the sharp front teeth in their lower jaw and the hard gums of their upper jaw. Food is ground up using the back teeth, called molars. Elk have two canine teeth in the upper jaw. Called ivories, they are the remnants of large tusks that prehistoric elk used for combat. The elk and the walrus are the only two North American animals with ivory teeth.

Elk are opportunistic feeders, which means they will eat nearly any kind of grass or shrub they can find.

At the start of winter, snowfall triggers elk herds to gather and begin migrating to lower elevations.

FAST AND FURIOUS

An elk herd typically uses the same migration route between its summer and winter ranges every year.

Elk are social animals that live in groups called herds. Adult males typically gather in bachelor herds, while cows and their offspring, called calves, form separate herds. Males graze in open grassy areas with nutrient-rich foods that help their antlers grow. Cows and calves typically avoid these open areas, where they are more vulnerable to predators such as wolves and brown bears. Bulls are not afraid, though, as they can usually outrun predators.

In summer, an elk herd may contain just a few individuals or more than 60 members. The herds travel from place to place, grazing on mountainsides. In winter, when temperatures drop to nearly -40 °F (-40 °C) and snowfall exceeds 30 feet (9.1 m) in some places, herds move to valleys. There they find more tolerable temperatures, protection from snowstorms, and easier access to food. Elk may travel up to 80 miles (129 km) to wintering grounds, following routes their mothers taught them.

Smaller herds often join together in winter, seeking safety in numbers. Winter herds may exceed several hundred members, providing individuals with a form of

Because elk can run up to 35 miles (56.3 km) per hour with excellent stamina, wolves typically give up after 300 to 400 yards (274–366 m).

In winter, wolves tend to stay close to elk herds, waiting for an opportunity to attack a weak or sickly individual.

camouflage called disruptive coloration. In these massive groups, the elk appear to blend together, making it difficult for predators to pick out individuals. Stragglers on the fringes of the herd are more likely to be preyed upon.

An older bull may join a winter herd of cows and their offspring, but most other bulls remain together. They usually rest on hilltops where they can see all around for a great distance. Their hearing is at least as good as a human's—maybe better. In winter, an elk's deadliest predator is a wolf pack. Most bulls can outrun wolves, but a large wolf pack can bring down a healthy adult bull that stumbles or gets cornered. Wolves encircle an individual, separating him from the herd. They grab him by the rump or back legs to bring him down. Then they bite his windpipe to cut off his air supply.

In summer, bulls begin zealously sparring. They entangle their antlers and push each other in a test of strength. In late August, bulls leave their bachelor groups to seek out cows. The strongest bulls become dominant, establishing territories and forming groups called harems by gathering cows and their offspring. Harems usually consist of 20 to 30 cows. To attract cows while

warning away other bulls, a dominant bull makes a loud, bellowing sound called a bugle. This call can be heard up to a mile (1.6 km) away.

The mating period, or rut, begins in early September and lasts about one month. The dominant bull will mate only with members of his harem. One of the male elk's mating behaviors is called flehmening. Curling back his upper lip, a bull inhales deeply through his nose. An organ in the roof of the mouth, called a Jacobson's organ,

Sparring may look deadly, but bulls' actions are slow and deliberate, with pushing and little or no bloodshed.

During the annual rut, dominant bulls spread their scent on nearly every surface surrounding their territory.

catches scents that are inhaled. The organ then sends messages about the scents to the bull's brain. This is how he tells when a female is in estrus, or is ready to mate.

To mark his territory and let the cows know that he is their leader, a dominant bull uses scent marking. He will spray urine up to eight feet (2.4 m), coating trees that he then rubs with his neck. With his front hooves, he scrapes out a depression in the ground. He sprays urine in it, and then wallows in the soaked soil, covering his underbelly, legs, and neck with the smelly mud. Bulls without harems, called rogues, constantly challenge harem leaders. They begin by making threatening gestures such as tearing up the ground with their antlers. Then they bugle loudly.

During a challenge, a dominant bull and a rogue will walk side by side in preparation for a fight. Then they clash antlers, pushing each other. The bulls may injure each other with the sharp points of their antlers, cutting their opponent's neck and shoulders. Battles to the death are rare. Usually, the weaker of the two bulls simply runs away. Because he is constantly defending his harem and mating, a dominant male spends little time eating during the rut. He may lose up to 20 percent of his body weight.

A dominant bull will sometimes mate with as many as 60 females in a single season.

In a show of dominance, bulls shred the bark off slender trees, staining their antlers dark brown with tree sap.

Yearling bull elk are called spikes because their single-spiked antlers have not developed forks yet.

By early October, bulls and cows once again go their separate ways.

After a **gestation** of about eight and a half months, a pregnant cow will find a secluded place to give birth. A single calf is born in May or June. Less than 1 percent of pregnancies result in twins. An elk calf weighs about 35 pounds (15.9 kg) at birth. Its coat is light-colored with white spots, blending in with the grassy environment. In addition, a young calf has almost no scent, helping it remain undetected by many predators. Born with its eyes open, the calf is able to stand within a few hours of birth and immediately begins feeding on the milk produced by its mother. The calf drinks about a quart (0.9 l) of milk every four hours.

After about two weeks, the calf follows its mother back to her herd, joining 10 to 20 other calves. The elk's excellent sense of smell helps mothers identify their offspring in the crowd. For the first two months of its life, the calf relies on its mother's milk, but then it grazes alongside her. Calves will gain 1 to 2 pounds (0.5–0.9 kg) a day, reaching about 100 pounds (45.4 kg) by the end of summer. Plant-eating elk require about 3 pounds (1.4 kg)

of food for every 100 pounds (45.4 kg) of body weight. That can be up to 30 pounds (13.6 kg) of food per day. When elk are not grazing, they are resting and chewing their cud. The first year is the most dangerous time of an elk's life. About 60 percent of calves living in bear and wolf habitats will not see another spring. Those that do survive may live to be 20 years old.

Although mothers keep watch over all the calves in their herd, each calf knows the unique scent of its own mother.

Created 700 years ago by the Anasazi people, Procession Panel in Utah depicts the migration of people and animals, including elk.

MAGIC, MYTH, AND MOVIES

Celilo, Oregon, was inhabited for 15,000 years—until the construction of Dalles Dam flooded the area.

Since humans first arrived in North America, elk have been important elements of people's spirituality and **mythology**. To express the value that they placed on the elk, many North American Indian tribes included the animals in petroglyphs, or rock carvings, and cave paintings. Such artifacts have been found from British Columbia to Maine. In Kejimkujik National Park in Nova Scotia, Canada, the Mi'kmaq people depicted elk in petroglyphs more than 2,000 years ago.

Perhaps even older are petroglyphs in the Pacific Northwest. For thousands of years, the area around the Columbia River in northern Oregon and southern Washington had been home to Warm Springs, Yakama, Umatilla, Nez Perce, and other American Indian tribes. In 1957, the Dalles Dam was completed on the Columbia River. It caused an ancient village to be flooded, and with it an area called Petroglyph Canyon, which contained thousands of images etched into the rock walls. The petroglyphs were so old that no one knows for sure which tribes created them. Before all was lost, several of the rocks containing artwork were removed and stored out of

Four arches made of elk antlers mark the corner entrances to the town square in Jackson, Wyoming.

Crow Indian wedding dresses are known to have been decorated with as many as 500 elk canine teeth, or ivories.

harm's way. In 2004, the rocks were put on display along the Temani Pesh-wa (meaning "written on rock") Trail in Washington's Columbia Hills State Park. One of the rescued rock images depicts a magnificent elk with large antlers.

In American Indian tradition, the bull elk represents masculinity and strength. His abilities to gather cows by bugling and herd his harem are celebrated in rituals and dances. Antlers were once used to make weapons, decorations, and medicines. The bull elk's ivories, which are much larger than cows' ivories, were highly valued by many indigenous peoples. Ivories were viewed as symbols of high status and superior hunting skills, and were traded, sewn on clothing, and made into jewelry.

In Lakota tradition, a man may harness Elk power— a magical spell that makes a woman fall in love with him. On a mirror, a picture of an elk is drawn and surrounded by zigzags. The zigzags represent lightning. Then sunlight is reflected from the mirror onto a woman. This flash of Elk power draws the woman to the man holding the mirror.

The first Europeans to arrive in the New World remained mostly because of the continent's abundant resources and potential wealth. Although fur traders

preferred beaver, lynx, and other soft **pelts**, elk were
also hunted for their thick winter coats. One fur-trading
company's records from 1787 show that 9,816 elk pelts
were exported from Canada to such countries as Belgium,
France, Germany, and Holland in that single year.

Elk were one of the most prominent animals
observed—and eaten—by American explorers
Meriwether Lewis and William Clark. From May 1804
to September 1806, members of Lewis and Clark's Corps
of Discovery Expedition killed 374 elk. The journals
detailing the expedition were bound in elk hide and
made 570 references to elk. In 1902, on one of his many
hunting trips to the western states, president Theodore

*Elk ivories have long been used to
decorate the traditional clothing of
native North American peoples.*

From HUNTING TRIPS OF A RANCH-MAN

Game trails threaded the woods in all directions, made for the most part by the elk. These animals, when not disturbed, travel strung out in single file, each one stepping very nearly in the tracks of the one before it; they are great wanderers, going over an immense amount of country during the course of a day, and so they soon wear regular, well-beaten paths in any place where they are at all plentiful.

The band I was following had, as is their custom, all run together into a wedge-shaped mass when I fired, and crashed off through the woods in a bunch during the first moments of alarm. The footprints in the soil showed that they had in the beginning taken a plunging gallop, but after a few strides had settled into the swinging, ground-covering trot that is the elk's most natural and characteristic gait. A band of elk when alarmed is likely to go twenty miles without halting; but these had probably been very little molested, and there was a chance that they would not go far without stopping. After getting through the first grove, the huddled herd had straightened itself out into single file, and trotted off in a nearly straight line. A mile or two of ground having been passed over in this way, the animals had slackened their pace into a walk, evidently making up their minds that they were out of danger. Soon afterwards they had begun to go slower, and to scatter out on each side, browsing or grazing.

by Theodore Roosevelt (1858-1919)

Roosevelt wrote, "wapiti [or elk] have a slashing trot, which they can keep up for infinite time over any kind of country. Only a good pony can overtake them."

Today, guided elk hunts are popular attractions in the western U.S. and Canadian provinces. Some ranchers even raise elk in captivity specifically so that they can be released and killed by hunters. Most hunting enthusiasts feel this practice of "canned hunting" is unsporting. Nevertheless, such hunts are extremely popular among inexperienced **trophy hunters**. But elk do not need to be killed for people to benefit from them. Since elk shed their antlers annually, there is generally no shortage of antlers to satisfy collectors and artisans. Antlers are commonly carved into knife handles, ornaments, lamps, and other home décor. Elk antlers are even sold as dog chews, and velvet and antlers are often used as ingredients in Asian folk medicines. As a fundraiser, the Jackson District Boy Scouts host the annual Antler Auction at the National Elk Refuge in Jackson, Wyoming. They typically sell about 10,000 pounds (4,536 kg) of naturally shed elk antlers.

Elk have also made their way into the media. Griffen Productions won a prestigious WorldFest film

In 16th-century Germany, elk antlers held candles on a Lüstermännchen, or "little chandelier man."

In the early 1900s, elk were introduced to Argentina and New Zealand and are now considered an invasive species affecting native plants.

In Yellowstone National Park and surrounding areas, motorists are required by law to yield to elk without harassing them.

festival award for its 2007 movie *Elk in America*. The documentary's highlights include rare footage of a cow giving birth and the mother elk and her calf surviving predators and crossing a raging river. It also features bull elk fighting for dominance and a wolf pack hunting bulls in winter. *Elk in America* was released on DVD in 2012.

Known simply as Number 10, a bull elk living in Colorado became an international television star when he was featured in "Showdown in Elk Town," an episode in the British Broadcasting Corporation (BBC) series *Human Planet*. The show explained how bull elk invade the city of Estes Park, Colorado, every summer in search of the female elk that live year round in the grassland surrounding the city. The show details how law enforcement officers and game wardens must keep elk and people from clashing. Tourists often try to get close to the visiting elk, which can be quite dangerous. After the show aired in 2011, fans followed the exploits of the bull elk known as Number 10 via local news reports that kept tabs on the animal. As an old elk, Number 10 was killed by a wolf pack in the winter of 2012.

Some movie elk are fictional. Four different prehistoric elk characters appeared in three of the *Ice Age* movies

from Blue Sky Studios, *Ice Age: The Meltdown* (2006), *Ice Age: Dawn of the Dinosaurs* (2009), and *Ice Age: Continental Drift* (2012). In the epic fantasy movies *The Hobbit: An Unexpected Journey* (2012) and *The Hobbit: The Battle of the Five Armies* (2014), the Elvenking, Thranduil, rides an enormous elk. The loyal animal also helps Thranduil in battle, using its massive antlers to trap orcs. And Thranduil's throne, seen in the movie *The Hobbit: The Desolation of Smaug* (2013), is made of elk antlers. King Thranduil's elegant and brave elk was inspired by *Megaloceros giganteus*, the **extinct** Irish elk.

The bronze-cast Wapiti Trail sculpture features five elk along an outdoor trail at the National Museum of Wildlife Art in Jackson Hole, Wyoming.

The Long Now Foundation is conducting scientific research that aims to one day bring the Irish elk back from extinction.

ELK MAKE A COMEBACK

Long ago, sea levels dropped and exposed land connecting Russia and Alaska; today, this land bridge is under the Bering Sea.

T he earliest ancestors of the deer family appeared about 40 million years ago. These were called pseudo-deer, because they had horns instead of antlers. As these animals' horns slowly **evolved** into antlers, the pseudo-deer became proto-deer, or "first deer." Proto-deer then evolved into many types of deer, moose, and elk. One elk ancestor, the Irish elk, was the largest deer to have ever lived. It stood nearly seven feet (2.1 m) tall at the shoulder. Its antlers spanned 12 feet (3.7 m) and weighed nearly 90 pounds (40.8 kg). It lived from 400,000 to 7,000 years ago throughout Europe and Asia. Scientists believe that **climate change** caused a food shortage, which ultimately led to the Irish elk's dying out.

The first humans to travel from Asia to North America did so by crossing the Bering **Land Bridge** 12,000 to 15,000 years ago. They followed animals such as elk that had traveled the same route thousands of years earlier. Fossil evidence suggests that elk arrived in North America about 40,000 years ago. They flourished—their range extended farther than any other member of the deer family. Scientists believe that more than 10 million elk were spread across the continent when European settlers arrived.

Like many other animals in early America, elk fell victim to overhunting. By the early 1900s, elk had disappeared from 90 percent of their original range. Once found from western New York to the Mississippi River, eastern elk were pushed into a small area of Pennsylvania's Allegheny Mountains. Deforestation and pollution had ravaged the elk's habitat, but it was overhunting that led to the subspecies' demise. In 1877, the last eastern elk was shot. The subspecies was extinct. The Merriam's elk once inhabited the dry landscapes of the American Southwest. But westward expansion sent people into the area and drove the Merriam's elk to extinction around 1906. The remaining four subspecies were dangerously close to disappearing as well.

By the 20th century, fewer than 100,000 elk remained. Yellowstone National Park and Wyoming's National Elk Refuge, created in 1912, offered some protection, but the herds had to be defended from **poachers** by armed game wardens and federal troops. Over the next half-century, the elk populations

grew, and more than 13,000 elk were taken from the Yellowstone and Wyoming herds and reintroduced to states and provinces where they had once roamed.

Carefully managed by wildlife officials, elk herds are strong today. About 100 elk travel back and forth between Minnesota and Manitoba. Roughly 300 elk inhabit Tennessee, and more than 800 live in Pennsylvania. With herds totaling 12,000 members, Kentucky now has the most elk of any state east of the Mississippi River. More than a half million elk inhabit the Rocky Mountains, with herds spread across Colorado, Montana, Idaho, and

Hunters in Colorado take more than 40,000 elk annually—more than any other state.

To help manage the elk population at the National Elk Refuge, about 1,500 hunting permits are issued each year.

Wyoming. The number of elk in the National Elk Refuge now overwhelms the available food supply. Because of habitat loss, the U.S. Fish & Wildlife Service provides supplemental feed for the 6,000 to 7,000 elk wintering at the refuge from December to April each year.

Elk are a vital link in the **food chains** of their habitats, particularly in Yellowstone National Park. U.S. Fish & Wildlife Service research has shown major increases in the populations of many scavenger species since the reintroduction of wolves to Yellowstone in 1995. This growth is directly tied to the wolves' predation of the abundant elk in the park, whose meat provides food for dozens of species in addition to the wolves.

Two studies led by researchers at the University of California, Berkeley found that wolves that prey on elk regularly leave their meals unfinished. This benefits other animals in the **ecosystem**. A wolf can eat only about 20 pounds (9.1 kg) of meat at a time. Even a large wolf pack cannot consume an entire elk in one sitting, so the prey is left to scavengers. Other large predators such as bears and cougars may guard their kill, but wolves leave their food unattended. This allows dead elk to provide food for a variety of scavengers, from ravens, magpies, and bald eagles to coyotes, pine martens, and wolverines.

Many current research projects involve studying the effects of climate change on elk. Climate change leads to warmer winter temperatures, which make elk more vulnerable to diseases and parasites. Pests that would normally die during the winter survive milder temperatures, making them abundant year round. One parasite is the meningeal worm, commonly called the brain worm, which grows in the elk's brain and spine, causing **paralysis** and death. There is no treatment for brain worm. Winter ticks are another serious problem. As many as 80,000 of these tiny bloodsuckers can live on a

Grizzly bears will eat anything they can catch—including elk calves and yearlings.

When resting, bulls in bachelor herds avoid eye contact with one another, because it can be a sign of aggression.

The western tanager is one of many songbird species that thrive in woodlands inhabited by elk.

Elk snort, grunt, squeal, whine, and even bark like a dog to invite other elk to play or to warn them to stay away.

single elk, driving it to scratch furiously on tree bark to relieve itching. Scratching all day instead of feeding can lead to weakness and starvation. The loss of insulating fur also leaves elk vulnerable to the cold.

A U.S. Geological Survey project found that decreased snowfall in Arizona's mountains has allowed elk to forage at high altitudes year round. This foraging has led to a decrease in important vegetation, including aspen and maple trees, which in turn has led to the disappearance of many songbird species. In 2006, the project fenced off a 25-acre (10.1 ha) area to keep elk out—just to see if the habitat could recover. It did. Trees, plants, and songbirds returned. So while elk are important to keeping many ecosystems healthy, climate change can actually cause elk to endanger a habitat.

Over many generations, elk have been woven into the fabric of North America's wilderness. They offer cultural and educational value to humans, as well as economic value, since thousands of elk hunting permits are sold each year, providing funds for many wildlife programs. Elk also help maintain the natural balance of their habitats by providing food for large predators and

small scavengers alike. It is important for people who share these environments to respect and manage both human and wildlife activities in order to maintain healthy ecosystems and wildlife populations—including the stately elk.

In places where elk are protected, they forage during the day, but otherwise, elk tend to forage before dawn and at nightfall.

ANIMAL TALE: THE NAMING OF ELKHORN CREEK

Appalachia is a cultural region of the U.S. that extends from southern New York to eastern Mississippi. Appalachian folklore is a mix of European and American Indian traditions with a strong biblical influence. This 19th-century Appalachian folk tale explains how Elkhorn Creek— an 18-mile-long (29 km) forked creek in central Kentucky—got its name.

Long ago, there was a beautiful Cherokee princess. She was fiercely guarded by her father and three brothers. But she was a curious girl and often wandered away from home to explore. One spring day, as she was watching a herd of elk, she spied a pack of wolves creeping along the tree line. Just as the wolves were about to pounce on a young calf that had strayed from its mother, the Cherokee princess jumped from her hiding spot and shouted, "Run, elk, run!" The herd bolted.

Angry with the princess for spoiling their hunt, the wolves turned their attention to the helpless girl. She scurried up a tree, but there was no escape from the growling, snarling beasts. A young Cherokee brave from a neighboring tribe heard the commotion. He hurried to see what was happening. Finding the princess, he chased off the wolves. Then he reached up to help the princess. When he took her hand, he fell instantly in love with her.

Day after day, the princess met the young brave in the forest. Their love grew deeper, and one day, the brave asked the princess to become his wife. She happily agreed, but when she told her father and brothers, they forbade it. "This man is not from our tribe," her father said. "You may not marry him."

The princess was heartbroken. The next time she sneaked away, her father and brothers followed her. When they saw the young lovers together, they drew their bows and arrows, ready to kill the young brave. Just then a great elk stepped in front of the princess. "You saved me when I was a calf," the elk said to the princess. "Now I will save you."

The princess and the brave climbed onto the elk's back, and the animal carried them away. But the princess's father and brothers would not give up so easily. For three days and nights they chased after the elk. Then, in a lush valley, they caught up with the elk, which had stopped to rest. Aiming at the brave, the men raised their bows and arrows.

The elk spotted their movement and threw himself down in front of the lovers, protecting them with his enormous antlers. But the arrows struck the elk's heart, and he died. Suddenly, the sky thundered, and angels came from heaven to carry the elk's soul away, for he had sacrificed himself in a most noble manner. Then the angels pressed the elk's antlers into the ground, making deep impressions in the earth. The princess began to cry. Her tears filled the channels made by the antlers, creating a wide, deep creek.

Upon seeing this, her father said, "Surely your union must be blessed by heaven. You may marry." And he turned away, taking his sons back home. The princess and the brave married and lived their whole lives in the lush valley on the other side of the antler-shaped creek—the Elkhorn.

GLOSSARY

appendages – parts that project from the main part of the body and have distinct functions

climate change – any long-term change of pattern in the planet's or a region's atmosphere, environments, and long-term weather conditions

ecosystem – a community of organisms that live together in an environment

evolved – gradually developed into a new form

extinct – having no living members

food chains – systems in nature in which living things are dependent on each other for food

genetic – relating to genes, the basic physical units of heredity

gestation – the period of time it takes a baby to develop inside its mother's womb

insulating – protecting from the loss of heat

land bridge – a piece of land connecting two landmasses that allowed people and animals to pass from one place to another

mythology – a collection of myths, or popular, traditional beliefs or stories that explain how something came to be or that are associated with a person or object

nutrients – substances that give an animal energy and help it grow

paralysis – loss of muscle movement

parasites – animals or plants that live on or inside another living thing (called a host) while giving nothing back to the host; some parasites cause disease or even death

pelts – the skins of animals with the fur or wool still attached

poachers – people who hunt protected species of wild animals, even though doing so is against the law

trophy hunters – people who hunt animals specifically to keep certain parts, such as the head or antlers, of the slain animal

SELECTED BIBLIOGRAPHY

Elbroch, Mark, and Kurt Rinehart. *Behavior of North American Mammals*. Boston: Houghton Mifflin Harcourt, 2011.

Fisher, Chris, Don Pattie, and Tamara Hartson. *Mammals of the Rocky Mountains*. Renton, Wash.: Lone Pine, 2000.

Jones, Donald M. *Rocky Mountain Elk Portfolio*. Helena, Mont.: Farcountry Press, 2004.

North American Elk Breeders Association. "Elk Facts." https://www.naelk.org/elk_facts.cfm.

Oregon Wild. "Roosevelt Elk." http://www.oregonwild.org /wildlife/roosevelt-elk.

World Animal Foundation. "Elk Fact Sheet." http://www .worldanimalfoundation.net/f/elk.pdf.

Note: Every effort has been made to ensure that any websites listed above were active at the time of publication. However, because of the nature of the Internet, it is impossible to guarantee that these sites will remain active indefinitely or that their contents will not be altered.

Elk are good swimmers and may spend time in lakes and streams to escape heat and biting insects.

INDEX